Greater Than a Tourist Book Series Reviews from Readers

I think the series is wonderful and beneficial for tourists to get information before visiting the city.

-Seckin Zumbul, Izmir Turkey

I am a world traveler who has read many trip guides but this one really made a difference for me. I would call it a heartfelt creation of a local guide expert instead of just a guide.

-Susy, Isla Holbox, Mexico

New to the area like me, this is a must have!

-Joe, Bloomington, USA

This is a good series that gets down to it when looking for things to do at your destination without having to read a novel for just a few ideas.

-Rachel, Monterey, USA

Good information to have to plan my trip to this destination.

-Pennie Farrell, Mexico

Great ideas for a port day.

-Mary Martin USA

Aptly titled, you won't just be a tourist after reading this book. You'll be greater than a tourist!

-Alan Warner, Grand Rapids, USA

Even though I only have three days to spend in San Miguel in an upcoming visit, I will use the author's suggestions to guide some of my time there. An easy read - with chapters named to guide me in directions I want to go.

-Robert Catapano, USA

Great insights from a local perspective! Useful information and a very good value!

-Sarah, USA

This series provides an in-depth experience through the eyes of a local. Reading these series will help you to travel the city in with confidence and it'll make your journey a unique one.

-Andrew Teoh, Ipoh, Malaysia

>TOURIST

GREATER THAN A TOURIST- SANTA MARIA SAL ISLAND CAPE VERDE

50 Travel Tips from a Local

Kirsten Waddell

Greater Than a Tourist-Santa Maria Sal Island Cape Verde Copyright © 2021 by CZYK Publishing LLC. All Rights Reserved.

All rights reserved. No part of this book may be reproduced in any form or by any electronic or mechanical means including information storage and retrieval systems, without permission in writing from the author. The only exception is by a reviewer, who may quote short excerpts in a review.

The statements in this book are of the authors and may not be the views of CZYK Publishing or Greater Than a Tourist.
First Edition
Cover designed by: Ivana Stamenkovic
Cover Image: provided by author

Image 1: By Daniel Åhs Karlsson - Own work, CC BY-SA 3.0,
https://commons.wikimedia.org/w/index.php?curid=32016869
Image 2: By Manuel de Sousa - Own work, CC BY-SA 3.0,
https://commons.wikimedia.org/w/index.php?curid=2831929
Image 3: By Cayambe - Own work, CC BY-SA 3.0,
https://commons.wikimedia.org/w/index.php?curid=18361428
Image 4: By Martikkk - Own work, CC BY-SA 3.0,
https://commons.wikimedia.org/w/index.php?curid=30903247

CZYK
PUBLISHING

CZYK Publishing Since 2011.
CZYKPublishing.com
Greater Than a Tourist

Lock Haven, PA
All rights reserved.
ISBN: 9798749823479

>TOURIST

>TOURIST
50 TRAVEL TIPS FROM A LOCAL

BOOK DESCRIPTION

With travel tips and culture in our guidebooks written by a local, it is never too late to visit Sal. Greater Than a Tourist- Sal, Cape Verde by Author Kirsten Waddell offers the inside scoop on the Island of No Stress. Most travel books tell you how to travel like a tourist. Although there is nothing wrong with that, as part of the 'Greater Than a Tourist' series, this book will give you candid travel tips from someone who has lived at your next travel destination. This guide book will not tell you exact addresses or store hours but instead gives you knowledge that you may not find in other smaller print travel books. Experience cultural, culinary delights, and attractions with the guidance of a Local. Slow down and get to know the people with this invaluable guide. By the time you finish this book, you will be eager and prepared to discover new activities at your next travel destination.

Inside this travel guide book you will find:

Visitor information from a Local
Tour ideas and inspiration
Save time with valuable guidebook information

Greater Than a Tourist- A Travel Guidebook with 50 Travel Tips from a Local. Slow down, stay in one place, and get to know the people and culture. By the time you finish this book, you will be eager and prepared to travel to your next destination.

OUR STORY

Traveling is a passion of the Greater than a Tourist book series creator. Lisa studied abroad in college, and for their honeymoon Lisa and her husband toured Europe. During her travels to Malta, an older man tried to give her some advice based on his own experience living on the island since he was a young boy. She was not sure if she should talk to the stranger but was interested in his advice. When traveling to some places she was wary to talk to locals because she was afraid that they weren't being genuine. Through her travels, Lisa learned how much locals had to share with tourists. Lisa created the Greater Than a Tourist book series to help connect people with locals. A topic that locals are very passionate about sharing.

TABLE OF CONTENTS

Book Description
Our Story
Table of Contents
Dedication
About the Author
How to Use This Book
From the Publisher
WELCOME TO > TOURIST
1. When I Say 'Tiny'...
2. Understand The History
3. Make Sure Your Data Roaming Is Off
4. Understanding The Money
5. Santa Maria Is The Place To Be
6. Check Out The Murals
7. No Need To Pack Your Sunday Best
8. If You Need Any Clothes Altered, Bring Them Along
9. Taxis Can Be Interesting
10. Be Careful Crossing The Road
11. Be Prepared For A Power Cut
12. Eat Like A local
13. If You Are Not A Fan Of Dogs, Eat Inside
14. Chicken, Chicken And More Chicken
15. Try The Tuna

16. Some Tips For Self Catering
17. Best View In Town
18. Fresh Fruit Smoothies And Your Next Instagram Hit
19. It's Not A Holiday Without An Ice-Cream Cone
20. Cape Verdean Beer
21. Feeling Brave? Try The Local Firewater
22. Order The Caipirinha In Brazillian Bar
23. So Much Beach, So Little Time
24. If You Want Pristine Perfection, Head To Ponta Preta
25. Respect The Ocean
26. Knowing Where To Swim
27. Bring Your Snorkel Or Rent One Here
28. It Gets A Little Windy
29. Don't Let The Breeze Fool You
30. Pack Extra Sunscreen
31. Keep Your Moisturiser or After Sun In The Fridge
32. Pack Towel Clips Or Weights
33. Don't Let Beach Sellers Ruin Your Vibe
34. Pack A Pic-Nic And Watch The Sun Disappear
35. From Shore Or Sea, Check Out The Surfing
36. Be Prepared For Creepy Crawlies
37. Don't Drink The Tap Water
38. Top Up Your Tan And Your Good Karma

39. Speaking of Turtles
40. You Will Need Closed Toe Shoes
41. Make Your Way To Serra Negra
42. If You Are Thinking Of Hiring A Car
43. There Is More To Buracona Than Just The Blue Eye
44. Take Off Ten Years In The Salt Lakes
45. Visit Some Of The Other Towns
46. When It Comes To Nightlife, Follow The Music
47. You Better Practice Your Dance Moves
48. Kizomba Hour
49. Learn To Play Ouril
50. Learning Creole = Earning Respect

TOP REASONS TO BOOK THIS TRIP

Packing and Planning Tips

Travel Questions

Travel Bucket List

NOTES

DEDICATION

This book is dedicated to my mum. Despite the distance between us, I feel you beside me in all my endeavours. I wouldn't be half the person I am without your unwavering support.

ABOUT THE AUTHOR

Kirsten is a travel fanatic and freelance writer born in Scotland who now lives in Sal with her boyfriend. She has been moving around the world working and looking for adventure for the past several years but has found home in Cape Verde. She now enjoys island life and loves baking, hiking and spends as much time as possible at the beach- leaving only for a cold beer with friends as the sun goes down.

>TOURIST

HOW TO USE THIS BOOK

The *Greater Than a Tourist* book series was written by someone who has lived in an area for over three months. The goal of this book is to help travelers either dream or experience different locations by providing opinions from a local. The author has made suggestions based on their own experiences. Please check before traveling to the area in case the suggested places are unavailable.

Travel Advisories: As a first step in planning any trip abroad, check the Travel Advisories for your intended destination.
https://travel.state.gov/content/travel/en/traveladvisories/traveladvisories.html

FROM THE PUBLISHER

Traveling can be one of the most important parts of a person's life. The anticipation and memories that you have are some of the best. As a publisher of the Greater Than a Tourist, as well as the popular *50 Things to Know* book series, we strive to help you learn about new places, spark your imagination, and inspire you. Wherever you are and whatever you do I wish you safe, fun, and inspiring travel.

Lisa Rusczyk Ed. D.
CZYK Publishing

>TOURIST

```
WELCOME TO
> TOURIST
```

>TOURIST

Beach in Santa Maria

Hotel Garupa, one of several villas in the west of Santa Maria

The city square of the city named (Praça) Marcelo Leitão

Aerial view of Santa Maria and the surrounding area

>TOURIST

*"People travel because it
teaches them things they could
learn no other way."*

- Jack Kerouac

Sal Island, Cape Verde is known by those who have experienced the joy of strolling along it's postcard perfect shoreline as The Island of No Stress. Spend a week or two here and you will have no doubts as to why. From the sound of the ocean waves mixing with local music playing in beach bars to the noise from fishermen in their brightly coloured wooden boats surrounding the pier as the market begins, every detail transports you far away from the worries and woes of everyday life and sets you free. I first arrived in this tiny paradise to a world of big shiny hotel resorts... but it was in the streets of Santa Maria, where true Cape Verdean culture comes to life that I fell in love with this unique and beautiful place. I hope the experiences I share with you now help you unlock the spirit of Sal and perhaps you just might fall in love as well.

Santa Maria
Cape Verde

>TOURIST

Santa Maria Cape Verde Climate

	High	Low
January	78	67
February	78	66
March	78	66
April	79	68
May	80	69
June	82	71
July	83	74
August	86	76
September	87	77
October	86	76
November	83	73
December	80	70

GreaterThanaTourist.com

Temperatures are in Fahrenheit degrees.
Source: NOAA

>TOURIST

1. WHEN I SAY 'TINY'...

An important thing to understand about Sal is just how small it really is. At only eleven kilometres east to west and twenty-seven top to toe- the majority of which is beach and desert- I'm not exaggerating when I say 'Tiny Paradise'. A lot of people don't realise this until they are coming in to land and can see the entire island out their window even minutes from touchdown. If you already have this in mind, you will be able to better plan your time and will get a lot more out of your visit. Because of the size, it is possible to visit most of the island in a day and some people might be disappointed if they are not already aware of this. I, however, believe this makes Sal a perfect destination for people who want to delve deeper into the history and culture of the countries they visit rather than scrape the surface and simply browse the touristic highlights.

2. UNDERSTAND THE HISTORY

The key to truly appreciating any culture is understanding a little about its history. Cape Verde, a collection of ten small islands, was discovered and colonised by Portugal in 1456 and remained a

Portugese Colony until independence was achieved as recently as 1975- something nationals proudly celebrate every 5th of July! While the unique blend of Portugese and African culture helps make these islands so special, it comes from many years of the archipelago being used as one of the most prominent transatlantic shipping ports during the slave trade. Cape Verde is now a proud, independent and democratic island nation and is the second country in history to graduate in 'developing' status according to the United Nations. I would urge anyone planning to visit Sal or any of the ten islands to read about the history so you can fully appreciate the journey made by this vibrant, unique and unforgettable place to become what it is today.

3. MAKE SURE YOUR DATA ROAMING IS OFF

I'm sad to say I learned this the hard way so please, let my mistake be a caution. Data roaming and international calls will rack up a painful phone bill in a very short space of time. Turn it off before you board and leave it off until you get back home, or better still keep the flight mode on to avoid charges

>TOURIST

for unexpected incoming calls and messages. If you need to contact anyone, try to use an internet based calling app as these are generally free to use. There are a few bars dotted around where you can connect to free wifi (Calema and The Brittania at Bailey's have two of the strongest connections) and almost every hotel offers this service to their guests. If you like to be connected at all times and are planning to spend a lot of time exploring, you can purchase a local sim card provided your phone is not locked to any specific network. You can buy one from CV Movel at the top of the pedestrian street and activate an internet package which should last a fortnight long holiday for somewhere around the fifteen euro mark. It is definitely worth it- using data roaming from your home network could surpass this amount in less than fifteen minutes!

4. UNDERSTANDING THE MONEY

The official currency of Cape Verde is the CV Escudo. This is a closed currency so you won't be able to get any before you travel. For convenience almost everywhere accepts Euros so if you have these you are good to go. Don't try to use any currency other than Euros or Escudos. Very few vendors will accept it and if they do you will not be buying at a good exchange rate. Visa cards work at all the ATMs but you won't be able to use an AMEX so bear that in mind if you plan to withdraw cash when you get here.

You cannot exchange Escudos back into any other currency so be careful not to take out too much more than you need. Make sure you have the right number of zeros on the ATM display before pressing confirm otherwise you will be left with unexchangeable currency that can't be used anywhere else in the world.

5. SANTA MARIA IS THE PLACE TO BE

Unless you are staying in a large resort hotel, chances are you will be based in Santa Maria. Although not the island's capital town, this is where the heart of Sal truly lies. You absolutely must spend time exploring this vibrant beachside retreat regardless of how comfortable your hotel may be. It only takes about forty minutes to walk from one end to the other so you can take your time and make the most of each day. It might be small but there is a lot to love about this stress free surfside hamlet.

6. CHECK OUT THE MURALS

Quite a large proportion of housing in Sal is in quite a run down state. Many families have made their homes in abandoned derelict buildings. In 2020, an Italian surf instructor who had been living in Sal for some time was moved to create Arte D'Zona. Through fundraising and local support she went from street to street painting houses and bringing life back into the backstreets. Alongside local artists she has created beautiful murals in some of the most derelict urban areas, transforming them into bright and vibrant housing who's residents proudly welcome visitors to come and have a look. When you are wandering around Santa Maria, look out for these incredible art works and multicoloured streets- or better yet, contact the group on Facebook for a guided tour and see first hand how something so simple can transform a community.

7. NO NEED TO PACK YOUR SUNDAY BEST

It can be tempting to pack your best shoes and flashiest outfit when travelling but trust me, this is not the place to bring them. The vibe is very much 'no stress, no fuss and anything goes'. The straight from beach to bar look is pretty common so don't worry about feeling underdressed. That's not to say you can't go full glam if you feel like it- some of the local girls get dressed to the nines to go for coffee. Roads in Sal are cobblestones and rough brick almost everywhere, so unless you fancy familiarising yourself with the inside of the clinic, please leave the stilettos at home. The same goes for men's dress shoes. After a walk through the sandy streets of Santa Maria, they will never shine the same way again.

8. IF YOU NEED ANY CLOTHES ALTERED, BRING THEM ALONG

If your favourite holiday outfit has somehow shrunk (or gotten bigger) since you last took it out for a spin, pack it anyway! There is a brilliant Senegalese Tailor near the pharmacy who produces quality work very quickly and is great value for money. As well as repairs and alterations, they have an array of beautiful African print fabrics of every colour imaginable and can whip up a one of a kind, made to measure garment for you in just one or two days. You can also bring in material of your own so be sure to leave some space in your suitcase for your new and exclusive items.

9. TAXIS CAN BE INTERESTING

You will find taxis passing by on all the main streets and can wave one down easily, in fact the driver will probably stop and ask you before you have the chance to raise your hand. You can also ask at the reception of any hotel to call one for you if you don't want the bother. There are no taxi metres, only fixed prices for journeys. No journey within Santa Maria should ever cost more than four euros- always ask the prices before you get in to make sure. However much you pay during the day, expect to add an extra euro at night- they charge for the headlights! If you are unlucky enough to be here on one of the few days a year when it rains, add another euro for window wipers... Crazy system, I know, but it's not negotiable. Also, don't be alarmed if your taxi has a bin liner as a window or the driver holds the door shut with a rope. At the other end of the spectrum, look for the pimped out blue fur dash and lava lamp gear sticks! Try to always keep small change and coins on you as taxi driver's don't always have change.

10. BE CAREFUL CROSSING THE ROAD

Traffic on the island is minimal, which is lucky as there are no traffic lights and next to no road signs. So, although the roads aren't busy, it can be a bit of a free for all for the cars that are on the road. There are zebra crossings dotted around but don't assume cars will stop just because they should- taxi drivers in particular pay very little heed to the highway code. It's easy to become complacent and expect empty roads, but many streets are narrow with views easily and often blocked by parked minibuses so make sure you double check before crossing.

11. BE PREPARED FOR A POWER CUT

One thing to keep in mind when venturing to remote African paradise islands is: things don't always work as smoothly as you may be used to, especially when it comes to utilities. For example, we experience regular power cuts usually with no rhyme or reason as to when and why but it happens, more often than not taking the water supply out with it. Don't worry, nine times out of ten they last less than a couple of hours, and if you are staying in a big hotel or condominium you may not even notice as they usually have a back-up generator which kicks in within fifteen minutes. If you are renting an apartment, keep a torch and a couple candles handy just in case. I've always found a candle-lit dinner with a head full of shampoo to be quite a romantic experience, and the unpredictability of it all simply adds to the country's charm.

12. EAT LIKE A LOCAL

There are plenty of pretty beach front restaurants with great food and crowd pleasing dishes but if it's a more authentic dining experience you are looking for, you need to head into town. Most of my favourite places are dotted around the more residential areas so my best advice would be to walk a few streets back from the beach and follow your nose. As lunch time approaches the smell of garlic, spices and smoky barbeque fills the air and draws you in. There are cafes which look more like somebody's house at first glance and are easy to miss so look out for sandwich boards advertising 'Prato Do Dia' and you will know you are in the right place. Why not try some of the traditional foods while you are here. The national dish is Catchupa which is a corn and bean based stew. They fry the leftovers with chorizo and egg which is a popular breakfast meal and will keep you going all day. Other local favourites include fried moray eel, feijoada and pastel- breaded parcels of spiced mashed potato mixed with chicken or fish.

>TOURIST

13. IF YOU ARE NOT A FAN OF DOGS, EAT INSIDE

The street dogs are a major fixture of all the towns in Sal and you are likely to find them everywhere you go. There are multiple charities working to re-home or provide shelter for as many as possible but this is an ongoing and formidable endeavour. As a lot of restaurants and cafes feed the dogs leftovers from the kitchen and many seating areas are outside, you will often look down and find a dog sleeping under your chair or looking up at your plate willing you not to finish your meal. If you prefer not to find yourself in this position try to eat indoors. Although cafe owners will shoo the dogs away if you ask, they will undoubtedly return soon enough to try their luck once again. Because the dogs are fed regularly by tourists and locals alike, you will find them to be friendly and curious so don't panic if one decides to join you on your walk.

14. CHICKEN, CHICKEN AND MORE CHICKEN

Grilled chicken leg is the lunch of choice for most Cape Verdeans, and trust me, they really know how to cook chicken! Everywhere you go will serve it, usually for a measly few Euros. It is mainly served with fries, rice and salad so is sufficient to fuel you for an afternoon of exploring. My top 3 grilled chicken spots on the island are as follows… Cafe Kriola on the main pedestrian street is one of the most popular cafes around and the spices they use are next level tasty. Cafe Fogo is a really local place near the police station and doesn't look like much when you walk past, in fact it's easy to miss. Their chicken, however, cannot be missed. They grill it on an open barbeque in front of you and the smell will have your mouth watering while you wait. My personal favourite is Restaurant Silva's. They have mastered the perfect combination of smoky flavour from the barbeque grill and mixed local spices which bring the whole thing to life.

>TOURIST

15. TRY THE TUNA

Sal doesn't have much in the way of local produce due to the climate but one thing it does have is fish. There is no large commercial fishing operation here so all the fish is caught by local fishermen in little wooden boats and goes straight from pier to plate all in a day's work. It really doesn't come much fresher than that. You will find tuna offered in a few different ways but I would recommend to try a simple tuna steak and ask for 'mal passada' which means it will be cooked rare. Beautiful. When it comes to fresh fish the best restaurants are the ones on the beachfront where you can see the pier the fish came in from that very same morning.

16. SOME TIPS FOR SELF CATERING

Renting an apartment rather than booking a hotel is becoming more and more popular in Santa Maria. If you chose to go down this route there are a few things to know about getting the most out of your food shopping. You won't find anything like the supermarkets back home and you may need to get creative with your recipes based on what is available at the time, but it's all part of the fun. The two biggest shops are Kazu and Huang. Conveniently, they are right beside each other and you are most likely to find the majority of what you need in one of the two.

For some things, however, you are best looking elsewhere. When it comes to fresh fruit and veg, I like to look out for street vendors. Watch out for the man selling from his wheelbarrow or the women with their buckets full of fresh produce balanced on their heads as well as makeshift stalls set up outside people's homes on the backstreets. If you don't feel like wandering around, the best place to go is the main market building in the centre of town where most locals go for their fruit and veg and is also where you will find the most variety. While there, you can also pick up some fish. If you are not quite up for the madness of the morning market on the pier, this is a great alternative. You will still be buying freshly caught fish, just in a different environment. Try the corvina fish, which is a bit smaller than sea bass but very similar in taste and texture. It's perfect for grilling with garlic or baking in the oven with veg and potatoes and only costs a euro per fish.

Lastly make sure to buy fresh bread. Although you will find a small selection of breads in the normal shops, nothing compares to a fresh out the oven roll from one of the bakeries. The most popular is Pao Quente- the only thing better than their crusty loaf is the cake! My personal favourite is Mister Pao, a small family run bakery in the centre of town just opposite the police station. This is a great place for coffee and a pastry, and the smell each morning really is phenomenal.

17. BEST VIEW IN TOWN

I'm a sucker for an ocean view. I'm a sucker for a crisp cold glass of white wine. Combine the two, throw in a guitarist, a singer and the sun on your back and you pretty much have my idea of heaven on earth. Odjo D'Agua is my idea of heaven in Sal. Originally a lighthouse, this boutique hotel and restaurant sits above the crystal waters of Santa Maria Bay and has not only one of the best chefs on the island but also the best views. The balcony of the old lighthouse structure remains as a walkway looking out over the white sand and on to the horizon. Take a stroll around here, drink in hand and you will definitely experience that 'No Stress' feeling Sal promises her visitors. You can often spot sea turtles swimming in the waters below and at the right time of year you may even catch a glimpse of a humpback whale! All year round you can look forward to a sunset which will make you stop and appreciate the moment. Odjo also has the only infinity pool on the island. Swim to the edge and you can feel the spray from the ocean waves below. If you are not a guest of the hotel you can gain access by purchasing a day pass wristband at the reception for under ten euros. Whether you stop by for a meal, a swim, or even to spend a night in one of its quirky guest rooms, make sure you visit before you leave.

18. FRESH FRUIT SMOOTHIES AND YOUR NEXT INSTAGRAM HIT

Cape Fruit is a quirky insta- worthy cafe hidden away at the far end of Santa Maria opposite Angulo Beach. Upcycled pallet furniture decorated with a mish mash of brightly coloured hand sewn cushions and hammocks hanging under wind chimes made from recycled plastics, help make this the prettiest coffee spot on the island. It also has one of the most vegetarian friendly menus and a really unique style of food. They have some weird and wonderful combinations but if you want something swapped out just ask- they are really easy going in that regard. Cape Fruit is the ideal place to stop in at any time of day: after a morning exploring the town, a midday coffee or for something fresh and tasty before you head to the beach. Be sure to order a fruit smoothie with soy milk, all the flavours are worth a try.

19. IT'S NOT A HOLIDAY WITHOUT AN ICE-CREAM CONE

Somehow, ice-cream just tastes better in the sun, racing the trickles as they melt down your hand and savouring the cold sweetness in the heat of the day. The best ice-cream is at Gira Mondo on the pedestrian street. They have a great choice of flavours as well as homemade frozen yoghurt and fresh fruit juices. They also serve good italian coffee, one of the best espressos in Santa Maria in fact. For those who prefer their coffee milky, order the Galao. Because it's located at the top of the main street Gira Mondo is the perfect spot for people watching, cooling down after a sunny afternoon or even as the sun disappears and the atmosphere changes- they stay busy late into the night for those who prefer chilling with a coffee to dancing with a beer.

20. CAPE VERDEAN BEER

Part of travelling is expanding your knowledge of international cuisines and cultures… but it's also about trying the local beer. In Sal this is going to be pretty easy to do as it's most often the only one available on tap. Strela is the beer of choice and the only mass produced Cape Verdean beer, so you might as well give it a try. There are a few varieties of bottled Strela, the most popular being 'Strela Classic' or 'Strela Krelola', the latter being the most commonly found on tap. The price of a beer varies from bar to bar, the general rule being the further you go from the beach , the cheaper it gets- although many central bars offer happy hours and weekend specials. You won't find much in the way of imported beer on drink menus, the only other common one is Superbock which you will find in most places as well as a few canned beers for half the price of a bottle.

>TOURIST

21. FEELING BRAVE? TRY THE LOCAL FIREWATER

The national drink is called 'Grogue.' Not very appealing I know, but when in Rome, right? It's alcohol made from sugar cane and if you try the real thing, there is no knowing just how strong it will be. One thing's for sure, it will definitely put a few hairs on your chest. Rumour has it, after five shots you will be fluent in Creole… if you are still standing! One of the most popular drinks is a Caipirinha- a cocktail using Grogue, sugar and lemon juice and you can't holiday in Cape Verde without trying one. A softer, but equally traditional alternative is Pontche De Mel, Grogue with honey. With a slice of lemon and a couple ice cubes this is a pleasant and refreshing drink for anyone with a sweet tooth. There are other variations of Pontche such as coconut, peanut or passionfruit, but honey is the most classic. For a good bottle of Pontche or Grogue to take home, local souvenir shops will often sell bottles. It's easy to tell by the labels which ones are mass produced and which aren't. I would recommend going for a homemade one as they taste a lot more authentic.

22. ORDER THE CAIPIRINHA IN BRAZILLIAN BAR

Aside from having the best caipirinha on the island, Brazillian Bar is one of the best places to be. Little more than a shack on the beach with wooden tables and chairs spilling out across the sand, Brazillian Bar embodies the 'No Stress' mantra of Sal. Located opposite the pier in Santa Maria Bay, it's easy to find and is a firm favourite for locals and tourists alike. One of their specialties is a 'Caipi-Black'. This cocktail is a twist on the classic caipirinha they are famous for with a splash of black vodka poured over ice with fresh lime- a deliciously sweet and refreshing beach side cocktail. Throughout the day there is a constant lively atmosphere which continues until a little after sunset. The hours will melt away as you sip your drink enjoying the music and the sunshine, people watching by the sea.

>TOURIST

23. SO MUCH BEACH, SO LITTLE TIME

Holidaying on a desert island means there is sand everywhere you look, so let me save you some time and break down the sections of beach I think are best. By far the most popular is Santa Maria Bay. This is the central area either side of the pier and it really is the heart of the town. This beach is best for people watching, swimming and its proximity to town. Pack your beach towel and water, find a spot on the sand and enjoy the sounds of Santa Marian life going on around you. This zone doesn't have many shaded areas but if you stay on the same stretch of sand and walk a little further to the right side of the pier you will find umbrellas and sunbeds in front of some of the more fancy beach bars. As long as you buy a drink you can relax here for the rest of the day.

Angulo Beach is quieter but still in the Santa Maria bubble and only ten to fifteen minutes walk from the central beach zone. I wouldn't recommend it for those wanting to swim as the water is rougher and beach rocky but if you are looking for some peace and quiet to read a book without having to go too far, the 'cheap and chill' surf bars here are a perfect place to relax.

24. IF YOU WANT PRISTINE PERFECTION, HEAD TO PONTA PRETA

By far the most beautiful beach in Sal is Ponta Preta. Ten kilometres of unspoiled undisturbed white sand and ocean views to take your breath away, this beach is pure paradise. It will take five minutes in a taxi from town or half an hour walk through the desert to get there and once you do, you won't ever want to leave. There is a small cafe where you can have lunch or a drink or get some shade but make sure you bring water and lots of sunscreen as there isn't much on the beach itself. The waves can get a bit rough here so be careful if you swim- you may just have to paddle, particularly in winter months. Depending on the time of year, you can see professional kite surfers from around the world training or even competing. In spring months you might catch a glimpse of migrating humpback whales and throughout summer the turtles will come and go. It's worth staying out until sunset as the view from the cafe with a cocktail in hand as the sun disappears behind the ocean is utterly breathtaking.

>TOURIST

25. RESPECT THE OCEAN

Be forewarned: although the ocean waters surrounding Sal are magnetically appealing and beautiful on the surface, the waves and currents can be fierce and must be respected. If you see a red flag on the beach, this means sea conditions are dangerous and you should not go in. Some people choose to ignore the warning but are doing so at their own risk. Please, be smart and don't ignore a red flag. The Western coast of the island is where the sea is at its roughest so if you are heading that way be careful. Not all beaches have a flag system and there are no lifeguards outside of Santa Maria so if you are not completely sure it's safe to go in, don't risk it.

26. KNOWING WHERE TO SWIM

The best place for swimming is Santa Maria Beach on either side of the pier. The bay here is more sheltered therefore the water is much calmer and it is more often than not safe to go in. You will still have waves to play in but currents are normally minimal. A good way to gauge the roughness of the sea is to look at the anchored fishing boats around the pier to see how much they are swaying.

Another good swimming spot which is a little quieter than the pier is the enclosed bay either side of Bikini Beach Bar behind the Melia Hotel strip. The further out waters can be a bit wilder but for a paddle in the shallow area, stone breakers protect the bay and the water is incredible.

27. BRING YOUR SNORKEL OR RENT ONE HERE

During Summer the water conditions are perfect for exploring beneath the waves. Warm sea temperatures and clear visibility make for ideal snorkelling or diving. If you have your own snorkel, the bay around Bikini Beach or underneath the Santa Maria Pier are easy places to get to alone, and the colourful shoals of fish under the pier really are beautiful to swim with. Renting equipment is easy and if you want to venture further out there are well priced tours available to take you to the best hidden spots. Ask about 'Christ of the Abyss', more commonly known as 'The Jesus Statue'. It's not far from the pier but too far to swim to unless you are very experienced. Because the statue is completely submerged, it's not so easy to find by yourself but ask about it with any snorkel company and they will let you know who can take there. If you want to push it a little further, you can learn to scuba dive even if you have never tried it before. If you already have your PADI bring your card and dive log to arrange more experienced level dives. Cabo Verde Diving is a reputable company with very experienced, patient and friendly instructors.

28. IT GETS A LITTLE WINDY

Although Sal enjoys an average 350 days of sunshine per year, the sun sets by around half past six in the evening so it's a good idea to bring a light pullover or jacket, especially if you visit during winter months. There is always a pleasant breeze, however December- February can be really quite windy at times so when the heat from the sun has faded, evenings can get chilly.

29. DON'T LET THE BREEZE FOOL YOU

So many people get caught out by the breeze and end up with some pretty painful looking sunburn. Cape Verde is near the equator and the sun is very strong, even on an overcast or windy day. Regardless of how the weather looks or feels, always put on sunscreen before leaving your accommodation and take a bottle with you in your bag. If you are swimming, re-apply every time you come out of the water and even in the late afternoon when the sun is getting lower, always have some for your face.

30. PACK EXTRA SUNSCREEN

Because it is so easy to burn and you will be applying sunscreen regularly, it's a good idea to bring an extra bottle because you will run out quickly and it is really expensive to buy once you get here. Even if you don't usually burn and usually bring tanning oils instead, bring at least one bottle of minimum SPF20 because you wouldn't be the first or last person to regret saying 'I don't need it, I never burn'.

>TOURIST

31. KEEP YOUR MOISTURISER OR AFTER SUN IN THE FRIDGE

After a day at the beach, you will feel the heat in your skin for hours after sunset even if you don't feel like you are burned. After sun or any aloe vera based moisturisers are the best solution and will help avoid skin peeling as well as helping cool you down. I always keep mine in the fridge rather than in the bathroom making them extra soothing and refreshing when applied. As long as you don't mix them up with the mayo, this will be a godsend after a day of tanning. If you get caught out badly, pure aloe vera extract is in a league of its own. It smells a little funky but is well worth it so you don't have to spend precious time indoors recovering from sunburn.

32. PACK TOWEL CLIPS OR WEIGHTS

Sunbathing cocktail in hand by the ocean or pool can become a lot less glamorous very quickly if you have to chase your towel along the beach or jump into the pool to rescue it. If you come during the windy season, be aware that winds can pick up suddenly and unexpectedly and your towel may fall victim to an out of nowhere blast. Towel clips are perfect to keep them attached to your sunbed or small weights for on the sand. If you don't have proper weights, find some rocks which will do the job just as well. It's also a good idea to have a spare towel just incase one does end up in the water, and generally speaking a spare is never a bad idea.

33. DON'T LET BEACH SELLERS RUIN YOUR VIBE

It can be annoying when you finally get comfy on the sand, settled in for an afternoon of sun only for someone to disturb you trying to sell to you. Unfortunately, it does happen. If you are approached by someone selling jewellery or souvenirs, politely decline and they tend to keep walking- if not after the first 'thankyou, no' then the second should do the trick. Promotion staff and tour companies are a little more persistent and will try to start a conversation. They are friendly, pleasant and just doing their job but it can be irritating if you are trying to relax. If you are not interested in booking anything, the best thing to say is: your partner (or someone who is not with you at that moment) booked the tours before you

>TOURIST

came, you don't know who with (whether or not it's true) and ask if they have a business card or leaflet. It works and can wrap things up a bit faster, letting you get back to sunbathing in peace.

34. PACK A PIC-NIC AND WATCH THE SUN DISAPPEAR

One of my favourite things to do is pack a blanket, pic-nic and a bottle of wine and head to a quiet section of beach just before sunset. The best spots are either Ponta Preta, in front of Angulo's or out past The Hilton because they are peaceful and have great views of the sun going down. Huddle up with your loved ones and have a toast to yourselves as the sun melts away and you feel yourself falling in love with Cape Verde.

35. FROM SHORE OR SEA, CHECK OUT THE SURFING

The Winter season in Sal (November- March) offers perfect surfing conditions and actually hosts the Kitesurfing World Cup around the beginning of March. This is a huge event for the country and creates a buzzing atmosphere around the island for the duration. Whether or not you are interested in surfing it's truly a great time to be here. If you fancy giving it a go yourself, take a lesson at Mitu's school on Kite Beach- appropriately named for the kites of every colour that fill the shoreline sky for a quarter of the year when beginners and professionals alike enjoy the waves. Mitu Monteiro is a Kitesurf legend, local icon and previous world champion, so where better to have your first lesson than his very own school. If you are lucky, you may even have him as your teacher.

36. BE PREPARED FOR CREEPY CRAWLIES

Tropical climates mean tropical bugs. We're not talking poisonous and scary, but oversized and numerous can make you jump all the same. Don't leave crumbs on the floor or they will be swiftly carted off by ants and any open food may attract other unwelcome critters into your kitchen, so keep it sealed or in the fridge. Pack some good quality mosquito repellent, especially if you are coming between July- October when the tropical season peaks

>TOURIST

and if you go out in the evening, pop it in your bag just in case.

37. DON'T DRINK THE TAP WATER

Tap water in Cape Verde is desalinated and although the systems are slowly improving, most housing and accommodation use fairly basic water tanks. It's fine for brushing your teeth, washing dishes or boiling water but for drinking, it can upset your stomach and just doesn't taste very nice. Bottled or bagged water can be bought from half a litre up to ten litres in any shop and there is a refill station in the main market with filtered fresh water. Refilling at the market is not only a much cheaper solution, but if you are out all day it means you won't end up with a bag full of plastic bottles. Aside from making your life easier and your bag lighter, reusing one bottle helps avoid adding to the plastic problem Sal faces with recycling facilities being extremely limited.

38. TOP UP YOUR TAN AND YOUR GOOD KARMA

Sal is known for its stunning white sand beaches and turquoise postcard worthy waters, but unfortunately it's not always easy to keep certain bays looking that way. Recycling and plastic pollution are fairly new concepts in Cape Verde and our position off of Africa's Western coast means some beaches have fallen victim to trash washing up on the shore. Sal is also one of the world's most important hatching grounds for the endangered Loggerhead Turtle so keeping beaches clean is a major focus. A great way to spend a morning is joining Project Biodiversity on a beach clean- you can contact the group on Facebook to find out when they are running one. It's free to join, they provide water and you will feel great about yourself having helped to make a difference.

>TOURIST

39. SPEAKING OF TURTLES

The experience of crouching on a beach under the stars, staring in awe as a 130 kilo Loggerhead Turtle hauls herself onto shore to dig a nest and lay her eggs is truly something you will never forget. Come to Sal at the right time of year and the opportunities to witness this incredible moment in nature will be endless. Nesting season peaks between July and October when thousands of turtles make the journey home to the very same beaches they hatched on more than twenty years earlier. Most eggs are laid late at night or early morning in the more quiet bays and although it is possible to drive out yourself and walk along the beach alone, the best way is to go with a guide. Try to book with a company which uses marine biologists. They will maximise your chance of seeing as many turtles as possible without disturbing or endangering the animals. Project Biodiversity run the bulk of turtle conservation activity as well as operating multiple walks every night and would be my choice of guide. If you come a little later in the season- September until December- you can see eggs hatching in protected hatcheries just outside Santa Maria and meet the tiny turtles before they are released into the sea to begin a journey of their own.

40. YOU WILL NEED CLOSED TOE SHOES

If you are coming to see the turtles, make sure to pack trainers or some good closed shoes as the walks operate at night and it can be tricky maneuvering an uneven sandy surface in the dark in flip flops. Wearing closed shoes will also avoid any unwanted collisions between toe and rock, something that would undoubtedly put a bit of a downer on the experience. The same goes for any desert activities. Be it quad biking, dune buggies or horse riding, closed shoes are a must for the safety of your tootsies.

41. MAKE YOUR WAY TO SERRA NEGRA

The landscape of Sal could be described as a sandy Mars. Areas of built up volcanic rock jutting dramatically out from stretches of desert, red dust swirling in the wind make parts of the island look decidedly extra terrestrial. Sal is very flat so any hill is bound to stand out but Serra Negra is one of the most beautiful spots. If you have hired a car and are planning to drive, make sure your car is suitable and won't be easily damaged. The best way to visit is on a

>TOURIST

quad bike or dune buggy. This way you can zoom right to the top and is a wickedly fun way to explore. You can also hike up, but be careful if you decide to walk out alone as it is easy to get lost. You can take a taxi out and the driver will usually wait for you for a small fee and take you back when you have finished your hike. The view from the top looking over the largely untouched East coast is spectacular and on clear days you can see the neighbouring island of Boa Vista. While you are up there, look for the stone piles at the edge of the cliff. Legend has it if you pile 5 stones on top of each other and they don't fall down, your time in Sal will bring luck to your life, so why not add yours to the collections of those who came before you and see if the legend is true. You can also zipline down which is an amazing experience for all the adrenaline junkies out there.

42. IF YOU ARE THINKING OF HIRING A CAR

As mentioned before, the island is not very big, but that doesn't mean there isn't a lot to see. Exploring the island is a must for anybody who comes here, and there are a huge variety of excursions on offer. If you are an independent traveller and don't really enjoy guided tours, car hire is a fairly cheap and easy option. There are, however, a few things you should know first. Once you leave Santa Maria at the Southern tip of Sal, there is one road through the middle until Espargos in the centre of the island. After Espargos you will find only dirt track and desert, so whoever is behind the wheel needs to be a confident off road driver. If you plan to explore the Northern half- and you definitely should- it's a good idea to choose a car with a higher suspension and/or built for rough terrains. This type of car won't be in the cheapest rental bracket but is far less likely to suffer damage underneath while you are driving, meaning you won't lose your deposit.

43. THERE IS MORE TO BURACONA THAN JUST THE BLUE EYE

One of the first things you will find online when you search 'Sal Island' is the Blue Eye. When the sunlight hits the water at the bottom of the cave, it looks like a giant blue diamond is hidden below the surface and is really very special to see- so special that many people fail to notice how stunning and

>TOURIST

hauntingly beautiful the whole area of Buracona is. Located on the rugged North-West coast, Buracona is a sprawling volcanic rock formation full of hidden caves and rock pools looking out to the atlantic where whales, dolphins and turtles regularly pass by. The restaurant has an ocean view deck and the seafood is brilliant so if you have the time, why not stay for lunch. There is also a great shop showcasing handmade jewellery and trinkets, clothes, grougue and all sorts of crafts from local artists and suppliers. There is a small entry fee but it's worth it to spend some time in this incredible part of the island.

44. TAKE OFF TEN YEARS IN THE SALT LAKES

Considering the name of the island is literally 'Salt' in Portugese, it should come as no surprise to hear that a large area of the island is covered in salt flats or salt lakes. The lakes lie at the bottom of an old volcanic crater near the fishing village of Pedra De Lume and are a natural spa, with the salt water and volcanic clay working like a classic spa treatment- although be warned, it doesn't smell as good! Best to go either in the morning or later in the afternoon to avoid the hottest sun and busiest crowds. Take some water, a towel and some small change for the entry fee. If you enjoy hiking, take good shoes and you can walk around the crater's edge- roughly a 4.5 kilometre trek.

45. VISIT SOME OF THE OTHER TOWNS

While Santa Maria is undoubtedly where you will spend most of your time, the less touristic towns are also worth visiting if you want to see more of the real Sal. Taxis are relatively inexpensive but you can also take the public bus for a euro to either Palmeira or Espargos. The bus doesn't run on any schedule, they wait until the seats are filled so you might be lucky and leave straight away but be prepared to wait a while.

Palmeira is a fishing town and home to the main port where there is always a hubbub of activity. Here, you can choose to head out to sea for the day on a sailboat or catamaran or stroll through the town enjoying a slower pace of life. There are some great little seafood restaurants and a street food market every Sunday.

>TOURIST

Espargos is the island's capital and where the majority of the population live. Nightlife is a big part of central Espargos with small bars dotted round the square, one of the best being Porto Cinqo. You won't see many tourists but don't let that put you off. Cape Verdeans are friendly and welcoming people and will make you feel at home. On the outskirts of town you will see a signaling tower on top of a hill. Walk to the top for 360 degree views and about half way up someone has painted a huge 'I LOVE SAL' mural which is a staple photo opportunity and one of the most famous spots. For lunch, Bom Dia Cafe makes a brilliant catchupa.

46. WHEN IT COMES TO NIGHTLIFE, FOLLOW THE MUSIC

Santa Maria nightlife is great, and one of the best parts is the live music. From late afternoon and all through the evening you will find a variety of artists performing both local music and popular hits. If you are out for an afternoon drink, from around 2pm many restaurants will have live musicians to entertain you until around 7pm when the bars will start with their acts. The most popular are based around the

President Square or along the main pedestrian street, meaning you can work your way along until you get to Buddy Bar. Probably the best known and most popular live music bar in Sal, Buddy's showcases the best up and coming artists on the island and is usually fully packed with patrons spilling out to the tables on the street. There is always a great atmosphere around Buddy Bar with people inside dancing while the band plays or outside simply enjoying the music and a chat with friends. Live music usually continues until almost midnight with the party going on late into the night should you want to stay.

47. YOU BETTER PRACTICE YOUR DANCE MOVES

Cape Verdeans are born with rhythm in their bones and music in their soul, so any open space becomes a dance floor. Nightlife in Santa Maria revolves around the music with the crowds moving bar to bar in search of the best beat and everybody gets up to dance. It's just not cool to sit stoically at the bar- it's all about letting your hair down, joining the circle and dancing like nobody's watching. Don't be afraid of looking stupid, there are no rules about how you should dance

>TOURIST

as long as you are having fun. Ocean Cafe is usually where the night kicks off, with staff leading group dances and getting the whole bar in the mood for a party. Whether you get up to dance or just to watch the very talented locals doing what they do best, be sure to get involved somehow.

48. KIZOMBA HOUR

Kizomba is an Angolan style of dance and music and is very popular throughout Cape Verde. You will hear Kizomba music playing often and the dance style is recognisable. It's very sensual with a lot of hip action and body rolling- the locals make it look easy but it might take a few tries to get the rhythm, but you will always find someone willing to teach you. If you are alone on the dance floor when the music starts, be ready for multiple offers of partnership- nobody dances Kizomba alone. If you don't want to dance with a partner, best to sit this one out.

49. LEARN TO PLAY OURIL

Walking around town you will see men perched on stools outside their homes or in front of cafes playing 'Ouril'. This ancient board game was originally brought to Cape Verde from mainland Africa by slaves and is one of the most popular pastimes particularly amongst the older generation. The board is made up of six 'pits' and each player starts with 24 stones on their side of the board. Rules vary depending on who you talk to but the basic idea is to end up with the most stones at the end of the game. You can buy your own set in any souvenir shop, usually made from beautifully carved wood and smoothed down pebbles. Take it with you when you go into town and ask someone to play. They will be more than happy to teach you. Order a couple glasses of pontche, play some Ouril and soon you will be accepted as an honorary local.

>TOURIST

50. LEARNING CREOLE = EARNING RESPECT

The official language of Cape Verde is Portugese but the spoken language is Creole. A take on the African Kriolu mixed mainly with Portugese sprinkled with hints of French and English, Creole is what locals lovingly call a 'catchupa language', meaning it has a bit of everything inside. It may not be the easiest to learn because there is no official written dialect but like most places, any effort to use basic lines and phrases is greatly received and appreciated. The more conversational basics you manage to pick up the better. In Santa Maria you will find a lot of people speak English excellently along with many other languages but at the same time others speak very little, so knowing little bits and pieces will come in useful. Locals love to see tourists making an effort to learn and participate in the culture, so learning a few Creole greetings will go a long way.

>TOURIST

To round off my 50 things to know, here are a few basic phrases to get you started.

Bom Dia/ Boa Tarde/ Bon Noite : Good Morning/ Good Afternoon/ Good Night
Tu Dret? : Are you well?
Sim. E bo? : Yes. And you?
Manera? : How's things? What's up? (A casual greeting)
Kuando es li? : How much is this?
Sim/ Nao : Yes/ No
Obrigada(o) : Thankyou- (a) for women (o) for men
Um Kray : I would like
Um Ka Kray : I don't want
Tava Muito Bom : That was great
Bo Tem : Do you have
Desculpa : Sorry / Excuse me
Por Fa Vor : Please

>TOURIST

TOP REASONS TO BOOK THIS TRIP

Unspoiled by Tourism: While Sal is always developing, the slower pace of life means it has not yet been spoiled by mainstream tourism. Local life and culture is still a prominent feature and everyday living shines brightly through the touristic aspects of the island.

Beaches: Paint a picture of the perfect beach in your mind and you will be envisioning any one of the beaches in Sal. Between the turquoise waters where turtles, dolphins and even whales can be seen throughout the year and the white sand bays where island life is at its best, beaches in Sal are hard to beat.

Unique Culture: Sal and all of Cape Verde is like nowhere else on earth and is a truly unforgettable destination. The rich heritage, history and diverse mixture of influences come together to make this island nation an incredibly special place.

\>TOURIST

DID YOU KNOW?

- The word 'Morabeza' is unique to Cape Verde and has no literal translation other than what it means to be Cape Verdean. It embodies the idea of hospitality, open heartedness and the laid back friendly spirit of the Cape Verdean people. The first hotel ever built on the island in 1967 was named 'Morabeza' to represent these values.
- Sal International Airport is named after Amilcar Cabral- one of the most important anti-colonial leaders and pioneers in Africa's history. The airport was also one of NASA's potential locations for the Space Shuttle to land upon its return to Earth.
- The population of all 10 islands combined is just over half a million, with only 40,000 people living on Sal Island
- The first ever African Beach Games, organised by the African Olympics Committee were held in Sal in 2019. The overall winning country was Morocco, with Cape Verde finishing in 4th place.
- There is only one species of animal that is actually native to Cape Verde- the Grey Long-eared Bat. Although the islands are a popular migration spot for many animals from both the sea and the sky, the

Volcanic soil and landscape makes it difficult for most animals to breed.

- All 10 islands are volcanic, but the only active volcano is the island of Fogo. It erupted in 2014 for the first time in 20 years.
- Sal is famous for its white sand beaches but in fact, if you dig deep, the sand is all black. This is because it is volcanic. What you see is a build up of the sand carried on the winds from the Sahara over many many years.
- There are no trains or railways in all of Cape Verde.

>TOURIST

PACKING AND PLANNING TIPS

A Week before Leaving

- Arrange for someone to take care of pets and water plants.
- Email and Print important Documents.
- Get Visa and vaccines if needed.
- Check for travel warnings.
- Stop mail and newspaper.
- Notify Credit Card companies where you are going.
- Passports and photo identification is up to date.
- Pay bills.
- Copy important items and download travel Apps.
- Start collecting small bills for tips.
- Have post office hold mail while you are away.
- Check weather for the week.
- Car inspected, oil is changed, and tires have the correct pressure.
- Check airline luggage restrictions.
- Download Apps needed for your trip.

Right Before Leaving

- Contact bank and credit cards to tell them your location.
- Clean out refrigerator.
- Empty garbage cans.
- Lock windows.
- Make sure you have the proper identification with you.
- Bring cash for tips.
- Remember travel documents.
- Lock door behind you.
- Remember wallet.
- Unplug items in house and pack chargers.
- Change your thermostat settings.
- Charge electronics, and prepare camera memory cards.

\>TOURIST

READ OTHER GREATER THAN A TOURIST BOOKS

Greater Than a Tourist- California: 50 Travel Tips from Locals

Greater Than a Tourist- Salem Massachusetts USA 50 Travel Tips from a Local by Danielle Lasher

Greater Than a Tourist United States: 50 Travel Tips from Locals

Greater Than a Tourist- St. Croix US Birgin Islands USA: 50 Travel Tips from a Local by Tracy Birdsall

Greater Than a Tourist- Montana: 50 Travel Tips from a Local by Laurie White

Children's Book: Charlie the Cavalier Travels the World by Lisa Rusczyk Ed. D.

> TOURIST

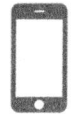

Follow us on Instagram for beautiful travel images:
http://Instagram.com/GreaterThanATourist

Follow *Greater Than a Tourist* on Amazon.

CZYKPublishing.com

> TOURIST

At *Greater Than a Tourist*, we love to share travel tips with you. How did we do? What guidance do you have for how we can give you better advice for your next trip? Please send your feedback to GreaterThanaTourist@gmail.com as we continue to improve the series. We appreciate your constructive feedback. Thank you.

> TOURIST

METRIC CONVERSIONS

TEMPERATURE

110° F — — 40° C
100° F —
90° F — — 30° C
80° F —
70° F — — 20° C
60° F —
50° F — — 10° C
40° F —
32° F — — 0° C
20° F —
10° F — — -10° C
0° F —
-10° F — — -18° C
-20° F — — -30° C

To convert F to C:

Subtract 32, and then multiply by 5/9 or .5555.

To Convert C to F:
Multiply by 1.8 and then add 32.

32F = 0C

LIQUID VOLUME

To Convert:..................Multiply by
U.S. Gallons to Liters............... 3.8
U.S. Liters to Gallons 26
Imperial Gallons to U.S. Gallons 1.2
Imperial Gallons to Liters....... 4.55
Liters to Imperial Gallons 22
1 Liter = .26 U.S. Gallon
1 U.S. Gallon = 3.8 Liters

DISTANCE

To convert ....Multiply by
Inches to Centimeters 2.54
Centimeters to Inches 39
Feet to Meters....................... .3
Meters to Feet 3.28
Yards to Meters 91
Meters to Yards 1.09
Miles to Kilometers 1.61
Kilometers to Miles............ .62
1 Mile = 1.6 km
1 km = .62 Miles

WEIGHT

1 Ounce = .28 Grams
1 Pound = .4555 Kilograms
1 Gram = .04 Ounce
1 Kilogram = 2.2 Pounds

\>TOURIST

TRAVEL QUESTIONS

- Do you bring presents home to family or friends after a vacation?
- Do you get motion sick?
- Do you have a favorite billboard?
- Do you know what to do if there is a flat tire?
- Do you like a sun roof open?
- Do you like to eat in the car?
- Do you like to wear sun glasses in the car?
- Do you like toppings on your ice cream?
- Do you use public bathrooms?
- Did you bring a cell phone and does it have power?
- Do you have a form of identification with you?
- Have you ever been pulled over by a cop?
- Have you ever given money to a stranger on a road trip?
- Have you ever taken a road trip with animals?
- Have you ever gone on a vacation alone?
- Have you ever run out of gas?

- If you could move to any place in the world, where would it be?
- If you could travel anywhere in the world, where would you travel?
- If you could travel in any vehicle, which one would it be?
- If you had three things to wish for from a magic genie, what would they be?
- If you have a driver's license, how many times did it take you to pass the test?
- What are you the most afraid of on vacation?
- What do you want to get away from the most when you are on vacation?
- What foods smell bad to you?
- What item do you bring on ever trip with you away from home?
- What makes you sleepy?
- What song would you love to hear on the radio when you're cruising on the highway?
- What travel job would you want the least?
- What will you miss most while you are away from home?
- What is something you always wanted to try?

>TOURIST

- What is the best road side attraction that you ever saw?
- What is the farthest distance you ever biked?
- What is the farthest distance you ever walked?
- What is the weirdest thing you needed to buy while on vacation?
- What is your favorite candy?
- What is your favorite color car?
- What is your favorite family vacation?
- What is your favorite food?
- What is your favorite gas station drink or food?
- What is your favorite license plate design?
- What is your favorite restaurant?
- What is your favorite smell?
- What is your favorite song?
- What is your favorite sound that nature makes?
- What is your favorite thing to bring home from a vacation?
- What is your favorite vacation with friends?
- What is your favorite way to relax?
- Where is the farthest place you ever traveled in a car?

- Where is the farthest place you ever went North, South, East and West?
- Where is your favorite place in the world?
- Who is your favorite singer?
- Who taught you how to drive?
- Who will you miss the most while you are away?
- Who if the first person you will contact when you get to your destination?
- Who brought you on your first vacation?
- Who likes to travel the most in your life?
- Would you rather be hot or cold?
- Would you rather drive above, below, or at the speed limited?
- Would you rather drive on a highway or a back road?
- Would you rather go on a train or a boat?
- Would you rather go to the beach or the woods?

>TOURIST

TRAVEL BUCKET LIST

1.

2.

3.

4.

5.

6.

7.

8.

9.

10.

>TOURIST NOTES

Printed in Great Britain
by Amazon